THE VICT(
AND EDWA
ON THE MOVE

John Hannavy

SHIRE PUBLICATIONS

First published in 2011 by Shire Publications Ltd
Midland House, West Way, Botley, Oxford OX2 0PH United Kingdom
44-02 23rd Street, Suite 219, Long Island City, NY 11101, USA.
E-mail: shire@shirebooks.co.uk . www.shirebooks.co.uk

A CIP catalogue record for this book is available from the British Library.
Shire Library no. 620   .   ISBN-13: 978 0 74780 820 6

John Hannavy has asserted his right under the Copyright, Designs and Patents Act 1988 to be identified as the author of this book.

Printed in China through Worldprint.

11 12 13 14 15 10 9 8 7 6 5 4 3 2 1

COVER IMAGE
Keeping a safe distance from the horse-drawn cab in front, and with not a motor car in sight, tramcar No 644 – introduced in 1901 – makes its way along Sauchiehall Street in Glasgow around 1905. The clock on the building in the middle distance, showing five past eight, identifies this scene as the beginning of the morning rush hour, yet the upper decks of the trams seem remarkably empty.

TITLE PAGE IMAGE
The High Street in Tenbury Wells, Worcestershire, c. 1902, with a typical mix of horse-drawn vehicles, handcarts and pedestrians, and not a motorised vehicle in sight. Tenbury Wells was, at the time, enjoying a resurgence of interest in its spa waters, and attracting growing numbers of visitors. Local photographer, Gardner of Tenbury, took the photograph which was published as a postcard by Valentine of Dundee.

CONTENTS PAGE IMAGE
This beautiful and rare ambrotype of a stable hand with his two carriage horses dates from the mid-1860s. The prominence of the figure of the stable hand himself is unusual. Clearly this was not intended primarily as a study of the horses, for in that case the stable hand would be behind the animals. And yet servants were only rarely photographed in this period, due to the cost.

Shire Publications is supporting the Woodland Trust, the UK's leading woodland conservation charity, by funding the dedication of trees.

CONTENTS

PREFACE

This is the fifth in my series of books looking at Victorian and Edwardian life through the images which have been passed down to us, and once again the majority of illustrations have been drawn from my own collection of photographs and postcards.

In concentrating on the developing transport systems of Victorian and Edwardian Britain, the subject matter is a little more focused than my most recent offerings – *Victorians and Edwardians at Work*, and *Victorians and Edwardians at Play*, and it picks up and develops some of the themes introduced in those two books, as well as the earlier two, *The English Seaside in Victorian and Edwardian Times*, and *Britain's Working Coast in Victorian and Edwardian Times*.

Once again, my thanks are due to the many people who have answered my endless questions, and especially to those who have alerted me to the availability of splendid images.

Thanks also to my literary friends who have pointed me towards engaging contemporary accounts of the development of transport systems on road, rail and sea – for it is those extracts from writers more eminent than I which makes these more than just picture books.

Finally, very special thanks to Kath, my wife, who came up with the original idea for this book, and set me off on months of fascinating enquiry.

John Hannavy, Great Cheverell, 2011

The Army Service Corps on Review, a postcard, c. 1905, from Max Ettlinger's extensive series 'Life in Our Army'. The Edwardian armed forces maintained and worked tens of thousands of horses in every aspect of their work, from fast light cavalry mounts to the heavy horses which pulled supply trains.

INTRODUCTION

Crawling along in my car behind a horse-drawn brewer's dray – itself a picturesque reminder of days gone by – was a timely reminder of what the pace of life was like on Victorian streets.

The speed of a walking horse dictated the pace of all the traffic in the days before steam vehicles and, later, petrol-engined vehicles were introduced, and the smell of exhaust fumes replaced the smell of horses.

Towns must have been a lot quieter then, and the risk to life and limb when crossing the road somewhat less than today. Everything is relative of course – the Victorian academic Arthur Munby, staying in a hotel in Wigan, Lancashire, wrote in his diary that the sound of hundreds of mill girls in their clogs was deafening as they walked up the cobbled main street – Standishgate – on their way to work in the mills which lined nearby Wallgate. Today, Standishgate is an exception to the rule – it is quieter rather than noisier now that it has been pedestrianised. But in the 1960s, when traffic ran both ways up and down the street, the noise levels would have considerably exceeded those which deafened Munby.

While traffic and people movement in early nineteenth-century towns and cities rarely exceeded that of the walking horse – exceptions being the emergency

This scene outside the gateway to Battle Abbey was captured in 1902, as the local hunt prepared to set off, watched by several groups of people from their coaches. To maintain the huge numbers of horses in use at the time provided work for tens of thousands of people across the country.

A busy scene on the fish quay at South Shields, c. 1905. Handcarts and trolleys were the usual transport used by the porters to move the fish from the trawlers to the auction shed.

services – the streets were also a lot safer, with stopping in the street to talk to a friend bringing no real risk. Outside of built-up areas, fast coaches linked population centres, but clattering and rattling over mostly unmade roads, locals could hear them coming a long way away.

In the days when the galloping horse was the fastest mode of transport, people's understanding of human ability to withstand speed was much less developed than it is today, and it was widely believed that travelling too fast could cause serious health issues, or even death. When the railways were introduced, scare stories suggested that travelling too fast in trains would cause breathing difficulties – a speed of 30 mph was even suggested as the maximum the human frame could withstand!

Improving transport systems gave people greater freedom to move around in the second half of Victoria's reign, but surely none of those who advocated the growth of railways, improved and macadamised roads, bigger ships and so on, could ever have imagined the far-reaching impact of these developments.

Left: A Lancashire lass going on holiday, c. 1908. Humorous postcards abounded in the Edwardian era, and proved very popular as more of the population enjoyed their annual seaside holiday. Railways linked even the tiniest villages, and third-class train fares were relatively low. Writing a postcard from the station to a friend was as commonplace then as using a mobile phone on the platform is today.

A group of fish porters from London's Billingsgate Market pose by a busy fish quay on the Thames before carrying boxes of fish back to the market. While the picture, taken before 1907, suggests they carried one box each on their hats, the reality was that they trundled heavy trolleys, each carrying up to six boxes, along the cobbled streets the short distance from quay to market.

While the movement of foodstuffs was restricted by the size of handcarts or the pulling power of horses, communities were much more self-sufficient. Food that was eaten locally was also produced locally, and the weekly produce markets held in just about every town across the land sold good food grown or manufactured within a few miles of the market square.

The canal networks had started the change in the eighteenth century, and the expansion of railways throughout the nineteenth century speeded up developments. With the ability to distribute goods more widely, and relatively cheaply, larger production facilities were commercially viable. Without the canals and the railways, the huge textile mills of Lancashire and Yorkshire, for example, would never have enjoyed the commercial success which they maintained for nearly two centuries.

Likewise, the wider distribution of food – together with such innovations as canning – came about thanks to the ease with which goods could be transported from manufacturing centres to just about every town and village in the country. The railways, as 'common carrier', developed a highly successful 'mixed goods' policy, which ensured that fish from Mallaig could be delivered fresh to London just as easily as two churns of fresh milk might be delivered to any town from the next village down the line.

Smithfield Fruit Market, Manchester, c. 1904. Horses and carts vie for space with the hundreds of baskets of fruit and vegetables which were delivered to the market from the outlying farms every morning before dawn. Much of the produce sold in this huge wholesale market was moved by porters and trolleys to the nearby Victoria and Exchange railway stations.

Wigan's Friday market – seen here in 1903 – brought hundreds of heavily laden horse-drawn carts into the market square. When the markets were discontinued, the square became a car park and bus station before being lost beneath a modern shopping centre.

A group of families from the north-east pose for the photographer during a summer outing. The photograph was sent from Hebburn to an address in Jarrow in early 1907. It was sent by Mr and Mrs McNeil to their friend Mr Giles, and from the message on the back it is clear they expected him to recognise several people in the picture – perhaps them, or perhaps even himself.

Sadly, we have no information on the setting for this group of over 130 people, nor why they had gone out for the day together – perhaps a works outing, or a church outing? What is certain is that a fleet of horse-drawn charabancs, like those illustrated elsewhere in this collection, would have been assembled to transport them to the location.

But, in order fully to understand how dramatic the change in transport was during the nineteenth century, we need only look at some of the contemporary accounts of life and work in some of the more remote corners of Britain. Writing in 1920, the wonderfully named Osgood Hanbury Mackenzie, then almost eighty years of age himself, recounted a story his uncle had told him of transport in the lands around Loch Maree in north-west Scotland during the early nineteenth century. The occasion was the cutting of the first sod of the first properly laid road in the area in the late 1840s:

> There being no need of wheels in a roadless country in my young days, we had only sledges in place of wheeled vehicles, all made by our grieve. He took two birch trees of the most suitable bends and of them made two shafts, with iron-work to suit the harness for collar straps. The ends of the shafts were sliced away with an adze at the proper angle to slide easily and smoothly on the ground. Two planks, one behind the horse and the other about half way up the shaft ends, were securely nailed to the shafts, and were bored with holes to receive 4-foot-long hazel rungs to form the front and back of the cart and to keep in the goods, a similar plank on the top of the rungs making the front and rear of the cart surprisingly stable and upright. The floor was made of planks, and these sledge carts did all that was needed for moving peats, and nearly every kind of crop ... The sledges could slide where wheeled carts could not venture, and carried corn and hay, etc., famously.

But with the help of government funding, which Mackenzie believed to be as much as £10,000, work started on the road around 1848, and was seen by all as a means of giving employment to local men, and as a vital step in opening up the area. It is remarkable to think, at a time when railways were already spreading across much of the country like a network of spiders' webs, and the age of steam was already developing rapidly, that there were still large areas of the country without proper roads!

Holidaymakers preparing to go out on a sail around the bay make their way down the jetty at Morecambe, c. 1906.

Two trams and a handcart are the only vehicles to be seen on King Street, South Shields in this view from around 1908. The No 2 route on the tram system had been horse-drawn since its opening in 1896, being converted to electricity by South Shields Corporation Tramways in 1906.

Mackenzie's book *A Hundred Years in the Highlands* is a wonderful account of the lifestyle and hardships in the first half of the nineteenth century, and contains some wonderful anecdotes. 'My readers will perhaps wonder how we got our letters before the Loch Maree road was made,' he ventures, and goes on to relate the perilous sea journey between Poolewe and Stornoway on the Isle of Lewis undertaken several times a week by the area's intrepid 'postie'. A network of coastal sloops brought in supplies as well as mail, and provided essential links with more populated areas.

The Mackenzies of Poolewe were wealthy landowners for whom travel was considered a rite of passage. They routinely visited England and France, and endured over five hundred miles of coach and rail travel just to get as far as London. Many of those who farmed their lands in the 1840s might never travel farther than a day's walk from home in their entire lives. Just how the nine-year-old Osgood felt about the long journey south from Poolewe to Normandy sadly gets just a passing mention in his book, as does his visit to the Great Exhibition in 1851, where the highlight as far as he was concerned was seeing the great Duke of Wellington.

Elsewhere in 1840s Britain, travel was rather easier than it was in Poolewe. Improvements in road building were easing the discomfort for long-distance coach travel on main roads at least, and while there was still no rail link across the border, the railway network was expanding. This book tells the story of these developments.

SHANKS'S PONY

For many Victorians and Edwardians, the cost of even the penny fare on a tram was a carefully considered expense. Walking several miles to church, a football match, or even to market carrying a heavy load, was not something which put off our predecessors. Nor did getting wet if, during that walk, the heavens opened. The wardrobe of even the humblest contained robust clothing which could withstand regular soakings.

It was not uncommon for the Victorians and Edwardians to undertake a walk of a mile or two each morning and evening on their way to and from work. Add that to very long working hours, and we get a picture of just how gruelling the working routine could be.

In cities, as in the smaller towns, walking to work was the only option for the working classes. In 1857, at the request of the Commissioner of Police for London, a survey was undertaken, reporting that over 100,000 people a day walked over London Bridge!

Left: Two Wigan Pit Brow lasses pose for the camera of local photographer Robert Little, c. 1870. Like most Victorian workers, these women often walked a couple of miles to work before spending their day screening and grading coal in the colliery yard. Some even ran home for their 'dinner' each lunch time before returning for a further five or six hours' work! In the published accounts of the lives of these hard-working women, it seems that getting home at 7.30 in the evening was not uncommon – and leaving home before 6 a.m. was the norm!

Opposite top: The huge workforce leaving the Singer factory at Clydebank at the end of the working day, c. 1904. Opened in 1884, the factory employed several thousand people by the turn of the century, and the sight of such huge crowds making their way to and from the railway station was a daily occurrence.

Opposite bottom: An equally large group of people have made their way to Newcastle's quayside but the reason for their gathering there is not recorded. With few vehicles other than trams on the road, crowds of pedestrians making their way to social, sporting or political gatherings were commonplace.

A march or a walking day in Jarrow, Tyneside, c. 1910. Marches like this were much less disruptive in the days before motor cars. Only the trams were seriously affected. It has been suggested that this march is either a Mothers' Union rally or a church walking day, and it clearly attracted a very large crowd. Certainly

the banner would seem to suggest a religious theme. Such pictures, printed to postcard size, were sold to the participants, as these were the days before widespread use of photographs in daily newspapers. Many were actually sent as 'personal' postcards to friends.

Believed to have been photographed in the east coast Scottish village of Auchmithie — traditional home of the 'Arbroath Smokie' — this delightful scene is entitled 'A Fisher Wedding', and was published as a postcard by Valentine's of Dundee around 1904. With not a vehicle in sight, it was customary for wedding parties to walk through the village after the marriage ceremony, accompanied by musicians, and invariably followed by the children of the village hoping to pick up some of the coins and confectionery which the bridal couple would scatter as they went.

ON TWO WHEELS

A group of cyclists poses for the camera outside Stirzaker's Bungalow, a curiously named cafe in Brock, Lancashire, 1906 or 1907 – and two more watch from the roof. Signs such as 'Caterers to the Clarion Cyclists Union' – a section of the Clarion Club – confirm that travellers on two wheels were guaranteed a warm welcome. As a sign of the times, the advertisement for 'Pratt's Motor Spirit' (top left) reminds us that there were already motor cars on the roads, although in this photograph the only vehicle in evidence (right) is horse-drawn.

Eleven young men take a break from their bicycle ride to enjoy a few beers – and to be photographed by the twelfth member of their group on 16 June 1907. Many cameras of the period took large postcard-sized photographs, so sending 'home-made' postcards was very popular amongst amateur photographers and their friends. The most widely available camera in the postcard format was the 3A Folding Pocket Kodak camera, introduced four years earlier in 1903 and remaining in production, through several models, until the early years of the Great War. It took a No 122 rollfilm, available in 4, 6 or 10 exposure lengths. Using the card to write to his sister and mother, 'M' told them that their chosen drink was 'Mrs Latimer's Hop Ale' which they had enjoyed after 50 miles of cycling. The card was posted in Heswall on the Wirral in Cheshire on 10 October that same year. We can probably assume that the cyclists were local men, although it is unlikely that they belonged to any of the major cycling clubs, such as the Clarion Club.

The bicycle was a creation of the Victorian era, and probably the best known of the earliest machines was the 'bone-shaker', a wooden-framed machine with pedals driving the front wheel, no suspension, and metal tyres on wooden wheels. The roads of the period were, of course, predominantly cobbled – hence the machine's nickname.

As with any new invention, claims have been made by and on behalf of several independent inventors – such claims usually made some years or decades after the event. One such story attributes the invention to a Dumfries man, Kirkpatrick Macmillan, suggesting he had built a mechanically propelled velocipede as early as 1839, although there seems to be little in the way of firm evidence to support his case. That lack of evidence, of course, does not seem to have diminished the story.

The pedal-powered bone-shaker first appeared in 1865 in Germany, just a few years before the famous 'penny-farthing', the first metal-framed bike. As the penny-farthing evolved through the 1870s, engineers realised that without gearing, the bigger the front wheel, the farther the bicycle would go on a single turn of the pedals. But the bigger the front wheel was – and some of them were very large indeed – the farther the rider had to fall when the machine hit a bump in the road, or any other obstacle. But, despite the risk of serious injury, penny-farthings were very popular, and so proud of their machines were early owners that they took them to the local photographer's studio, and had themselves photographed with their trusty vehicles. Such photographs are now highly valued by collectors.

Before the end of the century, chain-driven tricycles and bicycles were gaining in popularity – especially for ladies and children, as there was much less risk of falling off! An American variant on the penny-farthing was ridden with the small steering wheel at the front rather than the rear, and despite the height at which the rider sat above the ground, they became known as 'high wheel safety bicycles'! The design of the bicycle as we know it today had also evolved during the closing years of Victoria's reign, and cycling continued to gain in popularity as the twentieth century dawned. Some Victorian cycles even had gears.

Cycling clubs were to be found in just about every town and city in Edwardian Britain, and the health-giving benefits of cycling were widely promoted.

THE UBIQUITOUS HORSE

On the streets of Victorian and Edwardian Britain, the pace of life was dictated by the trotting speed of a horse and the walking speed of a man.

The horse remained the primary source of motive power well into the twentieth century, and to meet the demands of transport and industry, breeding and maintaining huge numbers of ponies, horses and heavy horses provided work for tens of thousands of people – including breeders, stablemen, grooms, drivers and, of course, blacksmiths. Ponies did all the hauling of heavy coal wagons down Britain's deep mines, heavy horses worked the country's farmland, and lighter horses pulled carts, wagons, taxis, early trams and omnibuses along the roads, and pulled heavy barges along the extensive network of canals.

In late Victorian times, horses and carriages could be hired by the week, month or year. In his 1888 *Dictionary of London*, Charles Dickens Jnr advised that:

> At the best West-End houses, a one-horse carriage (victoria or brougham) will cost about 30 guineas a month; a two-horse carriage, such as a landau, about 45 guineas a month. These prices, of course, include horses, carriage, harness, coachman, stabling and forage. In ordinary jobbing work a one-horse brougham during the day-time costs about 7s.6d. for two hours hiring; theatre and ball work cost from 10s.6d. to 27s.6d. according to circumstance and locality.

Such prices were clearly only affordable by the relatively wealthy in society.

Three horse-drawn carts make their way along Galgate in Barnard Castle, Northumberland, c. 1905.

At a time when the horse was the main source of motive power, the village blacksmith, like the miller, was a key member of the community. Here, the blacksmith stands outside his smithy in Gullane, East Lothian. As can be seen from the materials lying around the site, his forge was used to repair farm machinery as well as for making horseshoes.

The village blacksmith at Leaderhall, near Moffat, carries out running repairs to a horse under the watchful gaze of a pedestrian and a cyclist, c. 1906.

Two- and four-horse carriages laden with passengers are seen here arriving at Strathpeffer Spa near Dingwall in Scotland, c. 1902. Strathpeffer was the most popular spa in Scotland, great claims being made for the efficacy of its waters. The North British Railway laid on transport to deliver passengers directly to the spa from their specially constructed branch line station nearby.

Many picture postcards of the Edwardian era romanticised both the heavy horse and life in the country and on the farm, but such cards were highly popular with those who bought and posted them.

Horse-drawn milk floats stand on either side of Stirling's Broad Street, c. 1902, laden with their heavy milk churns. On the left, a maid has come out with her jug to purchase the day's supply. Horses continued to pull milk carts in many towns and cities until well after the end of the Edwardian era.

A heavy horse prepares to draw a fully laden freight wagon away from the goods depot at London's Camden Station, c. 1904, while an even more heavily laden wagon can be seen behind the horse. The station was opened in 1868 as Camden Town Station, and handled both freight and passengers. This photograph, entitled 'A Load of Manchester Goods', shows a one-horse wagon. The more horses the driver was in charge of, the more senior his rank. Known variously as carters, carmen, draymen or lurry men depending on which depot they worked at, they were all still considered as railwaymen. They worked 60 hours for 25s per week – a little more in London, Cardiff, Manchester and Liverpool.

Left: The stables at Edinburgh's main fire station, photographed c. 1903 and published as a postcard by Edinburgh publishers W. & A. K. Johnston Ltd. Edinburgh had the first municipal fire service in Britain – it was set up in 1824 as the Edinburgh Fire Engine Establishment, and was founded by James Braidwood, who is recognised as the father of the modern fire service. A statue of him stands in Edinburgh. He was the city's first fire chief, and later moved to London to become the capital's first fire chief in 1833 – he died fighting a fire in Tooley Street in 1861. The so-called 'Great Fire of Edinburgh' in 1824 put Braidwood's ideas to the test, and vindicated the City Fathers' decision to wrench fire-fighting away from the 'insurance brigades' – firemen employed by insurance companies, who normally only attended fires in premises covered by their own policies. The stables shown here were behind the main fire station in Lauriston Place – now the site of the city's Museum of Fife. Part of the stables has been preserved in a form not unlike that shown here.

Below: Sheffield's new fire station at West Bar, which opened in 1900, had three fire engines and stabling for twelve horses behind the engine-house. Six horses were kept constantly at the ready, two in each of three sets of stalls behind the engines. When there was a call-out, the horses were brought forward in front of their vehicles, and harnesses were lowered onto them from the ceiling. Snap-fix collars meant that the horses could be harnessed up to their machines and out of the station in a remarkably short period of time. The design and layout of the building was a great improvement – for men, machines and horses – than the earlier fire station at Rockingham Street, which had been the fire service's headquarters since 1883. Like in every other city, the Sheffield fire service in early Victorian times was supplied by the so-called 'insurance brigades' until the city took control of its own service in 1869 – the Sheffield Police Fire Brigade – and bought its first steam-powered pump in 1876. A quarter of a century later, when this photograph was taken in 1900, the equipment in use was largely the same. Here we see a horse-drawn steam pump on the left, a 'fire-escape' vehicle in the centre, and a general vehicle on the right. By the time this card was posted in 1908, the service had acquired its first turntable ladder (1903) and its first motorised escape vehicle (1907).

Working horses came in all shapes and sizes, the breeds classified in three broad groups – heavy draught horses, harness horses and saddle horses – each group valued for specific characteristics which were suited to the many different types of work they were required to undertake. Light horses and ponies were ridden and also used to pull light loads. For taxis, the Hackney was popular, as was the Yorkshire Coach horse. Hackneys were first bred at the beginning of the nineteenth century, crossing an old breed of trotting horse with thoroughbred stock, and they were nimble, well-tempered and fast when required to be. The Yorkshire Coach was a heavier breed able to pull larger carriages and light omnibuses, while the Cleveland Bay could be adapted to either harness work or farm work. For the really heavy jobs, three breeds predominated in Victorian and Edwardian Britain: the mighty Shire horse which could trace its origins back to medieval times, the smaller Suffolk which was bred in East Anglia specifically to work the fields, and the powerful Clydesdale which was bred by crossing local Scottish horses with Shires and heavy Belgian horses.

Charles Dickens Jnr was not a great supporter of horse-riding, urging his readers to take to their bicycles, and telling them that to do so would result in the saving of a lot of money 'to say nothing of the cruelty to horseflesh'. And there was,

In this remarkable postcard, photographed underground in a Wigan colliery by Thomas Taylor of Platt Bridge, pit ponies – who spent almost their entire lives in darkness – are seen with their handlers alongside the heavy trucks of coal they hauled along the mine's many tracked 'roads'. The horses were kept in stables deep underground, tended by farriers and stablemen. This postcard was sent from Wigan just after the tragic explosion at the Maypole Colliery in August 1908. On the back, the sender reassures his parents that he is safe, and tells them that ten days after the explosion, the wooden pithead gear has all gone, and despite the best efforts of everyone involved, the fires more than a mile below the surface are still raging. When some of the mines stopped work for their annual holidays, the horses were brought to the surface, but daylight upset the creatures so much that most were kept below ground in the near-darkness to which they were accustomed.

By the early years of the twentieth century, farming was becoming mechanised, but the source of motive power was still the heavy horse, and while large farms had their own, smaller farms hired these magnificent creatures when necessary. Some of the major players in farming machinery throughout the century were starting to make names for themselves, and what better way to advertise their machinery than the tinted postcard. This picture comes from a series of advertising postcards produced by the Chicago-based International Harvester Company of America in 1909. The company had the idea of showing their equipment in use all over the world, and this card, 'A modern Self-Binder in Bonnie Scotland, showing the famous Wallace Monument in the background', was photographed during the 1909 harvest on the rich and fertile farmland at the foot of the Abbey Craig at Causewayhead near Stirling. Given the location, the horses are probably Clydesdales.

undoubtedly, some cruelty to horses, but it was probably not widespread. A weak and emaciated horse would obviously be ill-suited to the tasks it was required to perform on the streets and in the fields, so there was a clear economic imperative in keeping the horse as fit and well as possible. That is not to say that horses did not suffer from exhaustion, as they were very heavily worked. The pair of horses that pulled a London omnibus, for example, would cover 50 or 60 miles in a day pulling their heavy load, and few operators used more than one pair of animals per bus or tramcar. Doubling the number of animals meant doubling the running costs. Unlike electric trams or motor cars, horses still needed attending and sustenance even when they were not working. A motor vehicle or a tramcar had much lower running costs after the capital outlay had been addressed.

But the gradual replacement of horse-power with horsepower not only affected the horses themselves, but also the many thousands of low-paid working-class people whose livelihoods were derived from taking care of them. As the horse lost its economic importance, so did the skills of everyone from the stable lads to the drivers. The former lost their jobs, while the latter had to adapt and acquire a whole new range of skills, or lose theirs as well.

A busy scene on South Bridge Street in Airdrie, Lanarkshire, dominated by John Young of Coatbridge's horse-drawn removal wagon. The heavy horse was at the heart of Victorian and Edwardian road transport – involved in everyday activities from pulling heavy omnibuses to hauling freight wagons and, as here, household removals. The weight of this wagon fully laden with furniture must have been considerable, yet only one horse was needed to pull it. Many removal companies were reluctant to convert to either steam or petrol-hauled vehicles – they were expensive to buy and, it was said, initially much less reliable than the horse. A significant proportion of small one-man businesses stayed with the horse until after the Great War. To modernise and adopt either steam or petrol power required a whole new raft of skills, whereas understanding the needs and operation of the horse had been learned and practised since leaving school.

Harvest time on a Scottish hillside, c. 1906. Two working horses are pulling an early mechanical reaper.

Coaches descending Yewdale Valley from Ambleside to Coniston in the Lake District, photographed by the Abrahams of Keswick, c. 1903. It took four horses to pull these heavily laden carriages, each with up to twenty-five passengers. On the steepest parts of the descent, the passengers had to get off and walk!

Above: Photographer Stephen Cribb produced a lengthy series of photographs about life in the navy. This one shows how big field guns were landed from ships, suspended between two of the ship's lifeboats. This card was posted in 1907. Postcards like this sold in significant numbers, to a nation still enthralled by the idea that the sun never set on the British Empire.

THE MILITARY ON THE MOVE

Throughout the Victorian and Edwardian eras, the British armed forces were engaged in either conflicts or policing duties throughout the empire. Despite being thought of largely as periods of peace and stability, Britain was invariably at war somewhere – or at least quelling some troublesome uprising or rebellion. Whatever the campaigns were called, they demanded the ability to get troops and armaments across the globe efficiently if not exactly quickly. The logistics of moving an army with increasingly heavy equipment around the world grew ever more complex as the nineteenth century progressed. It could take several weeks to transport the necessary men and guns to a conflict zone, and several more weeks to get word back to Britain if anything had been overlooked!

By the time of the Crimean War in the 1850s, a huge fleet of ships was needed to move men and equipment into place. While some were steamers, and many were steam-assisted – with sails as well as their sometimes unreliable steam engines – the majority of vessels in the huge fleet were sailing ships. So tightly packed were the predominantly wooden vessels in Balaklava harbour in November 1854 that when a

Main picture: Roger Fenton's study of the Artillery Camp outside Balaklava dates from spring 1855, and gives some idea of the heavy equipment needed for the war. Many of the great field artillery pieces were built at the Elswick Works on the River Tyne. Sir William Armstrong first made his fortune in supplying armaments for the British Army in the Crimea.

huge storm broke, they quite literally ground each other to bits. There was considerable loss of life, accompanied by the loss of a great deal of food, livestock and equipment still crammed into those recently arrived vessels which were waiting to be unloaded.

By the time Roger Fenton photographed the narrow harbour in March 1855 it was less crowded – he noted in a letter home that there were only 150 ships tied up – but he found a quieter corner for his first photographs and the same mix of sail and steam can be seen. Fenton had left the Thames on 20 February 1855, and arrived at Gibraltar a week later. The voyage to the Black Sea would take another two weeks and more.

As the army's equipment became larger, heavier and more mechanised, ever bigger transport ships became necessary, although these were invariably chartered from commercial steamer companies. Similarly, passenger ships were chartered to move personnel, so a war was seen as a commercial windfall for shipping lines as well as a logistical challenge for the military top brass.

Warships too were becoming larger and more sophisticated, demanding more and more coal to power them. Moving men and machinery around the world, therefore, required a huge network of coaling-stations just to keep the fleet moving.

In Edwardian times, with patriotism and unquestioning loyalty considered two of the strongest British characteristics, extensive series of postcards were marketed celebrating the armed forces and their achievements.

Previous pages:
The harbour at Balaklava, with some of the ships – a mixture of sail and steam – which carried men and supplies to the Crimean War. Most of the steam ships were chartered from commercial shipping lines.

Right: HMS *Magnificent*, built in Chatham Dockyard in the 1890s and armed on Tyneside. The 14,900-ton 'Majestic Class' battleship was a formidable fighting machine, with four 12-inch and twelve 6-inch guns, and a large crew. But she was one of the last of Britain's Victorian warships. By the time this slide was made, she was already out of date – the first of the mighty 'Dreadnoughts' had already been launched.

The Royal Scots at Rest – a postcard, c. 1903, from the 'Life in Our Army' series, an extensive collection of cards chronicling almost every aspect of military life.

Queen Victoria's army in the Crimea was highly mechanised for the period. Photographer Roger Fenton was surprised to find there was a specially constructed steam railway to transport supplies. By the time Fenton arrived, it ran 1.5 miles from Balaklava harbour to Kadikoi. 'Navvies and Turks were working together,' he wrote to his wife, 'loading wagons and laying ballast, and evidently on good terms with each other'.

From Tuck's postcard series 'Life in Our Navy', members of the crew are seen here carrying their kit-bags aboard a Royal Navy destroyer, probably at Chatham Naval Dockyard, c. 1907.

'Embarking Guns and Horses', card No 25 from Knight's series 'The Royal Navy', posted in 1908. The horses look completely unperturbed by the experience of walking the ramp to this fragile little boat. Once out at the warship horses and guns would both be winched aboard.

The launch of HMS *Lord Nelson*, 1905. One of the largest ships ever built at Palmer's Yard in Jarrow, she cost over £1.6m to build, and served in the navy for only eleven years from 1908 until 1919.

The London & North Western Railway produced an extensive series of postcards, not just of its locomotives and rolling stock, but of the construction and subsequent maintenance of the railway.

North British Railway locomotive No 405 and crew. This 1902 photograph was taken shortly after the locomotive, designed by Thomas Wheatley, underwent a complete rebuild at the company's Cowlairs works in Glasgow – it bears a plaque over the middle driving wheel to mark that rebuild.

THE AGE OF THE TRAIN

The 1830s and 1840s must have been exciting times in which to live. The rate of industrial progress was growing exponentially, and the transport systems which have been taken for granted over the past century-and-a-half and more were just being developed. In Newcastle, for example, a rail link to Carlisle was opened in 1838, lines to Darlington in 1844, north to Berwick-upon-Tweed in 1847, and south to London by the end of that decade. Before that, anyone going farther than walking distance would have had to use one of the many long-distance coaches which travelled along the less-than-smooth roads.

Stockton and Darlington were, of course, the birthplaces of the railway, and the north-east of England embraced the railway age with great enthusiasm – building many of the great routes which still exist today, but also constructing branch lines. The potential to ever make a profit from these, however, was only ever in the realms of whimsy! The same was true in Scotland and Wales, and the majority of the less densely populated areas of England. Many people lost a lot of money laying track beds which today survive only as footpaths.

But more than any other form of transport throughout the Victorian and Edwardian eras, the railways opened up the country for both commerce and pleasure, and introduced the population to the idea of long-distance travel.

The dangers of this new fast form of transport became apparent very early. At the opening of the Liverpool to Manchester railway in September 1830, William Huskisson became the first person to be killed by a passenger train. But he was not the first fatality of the railway age. During a blizzard in December 1821, a carpenter

The disasters of the railway age were long remembered – this photograph of the Tay Bridge disaster of 1879 was published in 1902 as a postcard by the R. H. Lundin Company of Dundee.

An assortment of London & North Western Railway coaching stock stands at the platforms in Birmingham's New Street station. This postcard was published around 1906.

Highly optimistic business plans drove much of the expansion of the Victorian railway network. There was probably never really enough traffic to and from Aberfoyle, below, to warrant the development of the Strathendrick and Aberfoyle Railway, which opened in 1882. The surviving postcards suggest that, for a time at least, there must have been: Aberfoyle Station appears in postcards, not in the monochrome or sepia of cheaper Edwardian cards, but in glorious colour! Coloured cards were usually produced in larger numbers to benefit from the economies of scale and keep unit costs as low as practicable. While locals did use the line, the majority of its passengers were met by fleets of horse-drawn charabancs for the journey to Loch Katrine's Trossachs Pier to board the steamers *Rob Roy* (until 1902) and thereafter *Sir Walter Scott*. The line was one of the first casualties of nationalisation in 1948, eventually closing in 1951.

Another view of Birmingham New Street with two of the 2-4-2 tank engines that shunted coaches in the station. 220 of these Webb-designed locomotives were built between 1879 and 1898.

In this lovely photograph from *c.* 1903, three different forms of transport have been brought together at level crossing gates. The steam engine, the bicycle and the horse were the most frequently employed forms of motive power throughout the Edwardian years, the motor car remaining a marginal and expensive alternative open only to the relatively wealthy. This scene was captured at Copnor Crossing on the London Brighton & South Coast Railway between Portsmouth and Havant. Nearby is Station Road, although Copnor never did get a station. A few years after this picture was taken, with both road and rail traffic increasing, the level crossing – with its adjacent signal box – was replaced by a bridge in 1910. The photograph was published as a postcard by J. Welch & Sons of Portsmouth and printed in Belgium.

The worst railway accident in Edwardian Essex happened on 1 September 1905 when the fourteen-coach Cromer Express derailed while speeding through Witham Station on the Great Eastern Railway. Ten passengers and a porter were killed, and seventy-one passengers injured.

Passengers waiting for their train at Northwich Station in Cheshire, c. 1907. The station was opened as part of the Cheshire Midland Railway in 1863, with the line extended to Chester in 1874.

A small tank engine pulls a mixed freight train across the viaduct at Aberbargoed near Caerphilly, South Wales, past the colliery railway yard. Opened in 1897, Aberbargoed's colliery, at its peak in 1907, produced over 4,000 tons of coal in a single shift, and would later have the biggest colliery waste tip in Europe. This 1906 postcard view shows an unusually quiet day in the coal sidings.

The largest railway junction in the world, outside Newcastle Central Station. Looking towards the station, the tracks for the suburban electric service introduced in 1904 can be seen entering the station at the right. This postcard was published c. 1910.

by the name of David Brook was killed by a locomotive while walking home along the track of the Middleton Railway in Yorkshire, and in 1827, local newspapers reported the death of a blind beggar, struck by a locomotive in Eaglescliffe on Teesside. Despite those early setbacks, development of the railways continued throughout the nineteenth century at a furious pace, with over 20,000 miles of track operational by the end of the Edwardian era.

Amazingly, over one thousand companies had been formed to build the network – an average of only 20 miles per company! The largest infrastructure project of the nineteenth century had been undertaken with no master plan, and no central guiding influence. Every new stretch of track had required an Act of Parliament to authorise it, but no central overview of the commercial or social viability of each line was ever required. By the outbreak of the Great War, amalgamations, takeovers and closures had reduced the number of companies to around 150. By then 4,000 miles had already been abandoned, and by the time Dr Richard Beeching had wielded his axe in the 1960s, the total mileage of track had been cut to 12,000, and the number of stations reduced from a high of nearly 7,500 in 1900 to fewer than 3,000.

Now moves are being made across the country to bring a number of stations back to service – and even to open some new ones.

One of Aberdeen photographer George Washington Wilson's views of Edinburgh's Old Town included this detail of early railway rolling stock standing in the sidings at the approach to Waverley Station. This detail is from a stereoscopic (3D) view card from the late 1850s. Over the following decades, Waverley was extended several times, with new tunnels dug beneath the Mound to access it. To the left, tracks ran through the tunnels into the station, and then south towards Berwick-upon-Tweed.

THE ELECTRIC TRAIN

If you had been given a business card by the Victorian Robert Davidson, it would have read 'Father of the Electric Locomotive', a rather ambitious claim based on the Aberdeen engineer's first successful experiment running an electric engine in 1836, and his first successful running of an electric locomotive on the Edinburgh and Glasgow Railway in 1843. The battery-powered engine could run at 4 mph, but did not have enough power to pull any trucks or coaches, and it was later proved that the cost of running the zinc-acid batteries was greater than the cost of burning coal. Almost forty years would elapse before the first true electric train ran in Germany in 1879.

Britain was rather slow off the mark in electrification, with the first electric train running on the London Underground in 1890, followed three years later by Liverpool's famous Overhead Railway – this used a 600v four-rail system, planning approval having expressly forbidden the use of coal due to the fact that the railway passed very close to the docks where many inflammable cargoes were handled. Newcastle's electric trains, using a three-rail system, opened in the same year, and in 1904 the Liverpool to Southport line was electrified using 630v – often described as the first British mainline electric service.

After that, with huge advances in the power of electric motors, numerous electric lines were opened, but electric railways subsequently evolved using AC rather than DC systems with either third rail or overhead pickups.

The Metropolitan Railway's Westinghouse electric locomotive No 1 at the head of a Harrow-bound train in 1906. Westinghouse supplied ten of these 50-ton 800 horsepower engines in early 1905 and the carriages were made for the Metropolitan by the Ashbury Railway Carriage & Iron Company of Belle Vue in Manchester. The Uxbridge to Harrow line opened in mid-1904, and for the first six months the trains were steam-hauled. These powerful electric engines were introduced on to the service in January 1905. The locomotives displayed what was then a novel roller-blind destination indicator.

An electric train passes a steam train in 1905, just outside Newcastle Central Station in another view of the biggest railway crossing in the world. The suburban electric trains running between Newcastle and Tynemouth had been introduced in the previous year.

Seen here, c. 1908, Marcus Volk's Electric Railway has operated along the seafront at Brighton since it first opened in 1883. It now proudly claims to be the oldest working electric railway in the world.

Above: Early electric tube trains on the Central London Railway – now part of the Central Line – were pulled by locomotives, each of which weighed in at a hefty 48 tons, and from the outset caused considerable problems with vibration. The entire fleet had been replaced by multiple units before the end of 1903.

Below: The Great Northern, Piccadilly, and Brompton Electric Railway, from Hammersmith to Finsbury Park, opened in 1906, and the event was commemorated with a series of postcards showing the railway, its stations and its construction. According to the company, the new line 'supplies the long felt want of a connecting link between the West and North of London. It runs through the heart of the Theatre area, and serves the West End Shopping Districts.' Here we see the 'Greathead Shield' used in the construction of the tunnel. Designed by James Henry Greathead, the shield, moved forward by compressed air and hydraulic jacks, was used from 1890 in the cutting of all the deep tunnels.

GOING UNDERGROUND

The world's first underground railway opened in London in 1863. The Metropolitan Railway's first underground line ran from Bishop's Road, Paddington, to Farringdon Street and, of course, the trains were hauled by steam locomotives, so the journey was often a less than pleasant experience.

By the time Charles Dickens Jnr compiled his 1888 *Dictionary of London*, the network was extensive and, for the benefit of his readers, outlining the listing of the system, he wrote:

> Recent years have seen considerable development, and especially in what is commonly
> called the 'Underground' Railway, a term which originated with the construction
> (entirely in tunnels beneath the Marylebone and Euston rds) of the line between
> Farringdon-st and Bishop's-rd, the first of its kind in the world; but a term, however,
> now falling rapidly into disuse owing to the numerous suburban branches which
> have since been constructed … These particular systems are, however, of such vast
> importance to Londoners – as is evidenced by the number of passengers carried by
> them annually, which reached in 1884 to the enormous figure of over 110,000,000.

That figure has today increased more than ten-fold, to well over 1.1 billion journeys a year!

Liverpool opened its first section of underground railway beneath the Mersey in 1906, ten years after Glasgow's 6.5-mile circular Subway opened – the only underground railway in the world ever to be conceived as a cable-hauled system – and it remained cable-hauled until 1935 when it was electrified and renamed the 'Underground'. Today it is known as the Subway.

The interior of a Central London Railway underground carriage, 1900, showing the armchair comfort offered to travellers. The line opened for service on 30 July 1900 between Shepherd's Bush and Bank.

UNDER SAIL

A small group of holidaymakers sets out on a short cruise under sail from Ramsgate harbour, c. 1905.

A mixture of sail and steamships lined up in Ardrossan Docks, still a busy commercial port in the Edwardian era. In mid-Victorian times the port had hosted regular sailing to Fleetwood in Lancashire, and to Ireland, as well as being a regular port of call for the growing network of Clyde steamers.

The Albert Edward Dock at North Shields. What writers often referred to as 'the forest of masts' was typical of Victorian docks. This picture from the 1890s was published as a postcard, *c.* 1904.

At Port St Mary on the Isle of Man around the same period, the shapes and tones of sails drying in the wind while the ships lay grounded at low tide proved irresistible to the photographer.

The tiny harbour at Charlestown in Cornwall at low tide, the ships safely behind the lock gates. These sailing ships, photographed c. 1900, worked coastal routes and cross-Channel routes to France. The majority of their cargo was tin and clay from Cornish mines.

This beautifully tinted view, looking more like a painting than a photograph, shows Sunderland Docks at the beginning of the twentieth century. In the midst of all the sailing ships, a solitary steamer is moored and, at the extreme left of the picture, we can see the paddle-box of one of the port's tugs.

A small fishing smack makes its way into Folkestone harbour under sail in 1903. Two large paddle steamers remind us that most larger vessels were steam-powered by this date, but many fishermen stayed with their traditional sailing smacks until after the Great War.

Sail and steam ships line the quayside at Newcastle-upon-Tyne, c. 1904. Many of these sailing vessels worked routes up into the Baltic and to the ports of northern Europe, as well as handling a large tonnage of British coastal trade.

Leith Docks – this photograph from the 1880s was published as a vignetted undivided back postcard before 1902, with this beautifully tinted version following in 1905. A single steamer is moored amongst the sailing ships, and a small steam-powered lighter is working in the foreground. Sailing vessels continued to be used on coastal trading routes, and between Leith and Scandinavia, so this image was probably still quite typical of the scene in Leith's older docks.

The Fife port of Methil was once the most important coal port on the east coast of Scotland, and through its docks, the Fife Coal Company exported millions of tons of coal to Europe and Scandinavia. At the time this photograph was taken, around 1902, the port was already exporting nearly two million tons annually. That would rise to a peak of over three million in the 1920s. The steamer at the right near the coal-loading gantry was registered in Sundsvall on the west coast of Sweden. At the time this photograph was taken, Methil operated two docks – No 1 dock opened in 1887, with No 2 following in 1900. The huge No 3 dock did not open until 1913, and despite the coal market growing substantially, the dock never reached its planned full capacity. Today No 3 dock has been partially filled in and is earmarked for housing. The other two docks stand empty most of the time, visited only by the occasional small vessel delivering timber from Norway and Sweden.

'The London Dock', wrote Henry Mayhew in his 1861 work *London Labour and the London Poor*, 'can accommodate 500 ships, and the warehouses will contain 232,000 tons of goods.' He went on to describe the sheer scale of the place – which was, after all, at the heart of Britain's trading power. 'The tobacco warehouses, alone cover five acres of ground. The wall surrounding the dock cost 65,000*l* [the '£' sign was not then in common use]. One of the wine vaults has an area of seven acres, and in the whole of them there is room for stowing 60,000 pipes of wine.' A 'pipe' could contain anything between 430 and 620 litres of Marsala or Madeira wine, and the Portuguese 'pipe' in which port was measured was 550 litres. Mayhew's description of the docks captures a real sense of the bustle of the place, and would have been replicated in any number of docks around the coast of Victorian Britain:

> As you enter the dock the sight of the forest of masts in the distance, and the tall chimneys vomiting clouds of black smoke, and the many coloured flags flying in the air, has a most peculiar effect; while the sheds with the monster wheels arching through the roofs look like the paddle-boxes of huge steamers. Along the quay you see, now men with their faces blue with indigo, and now gaugers, with their long brass-tipped rule dripping with spirit from the cask they have been probing. Then come a group of flaxen-haired sailors chattering German; and next a black sailor, with a cotton handkerchief twisted turban-like round his head. Presently a blue-smocked butcher, with fresh meat and a bunch of cabbages on a tray on his shoulder; and shortly afterwards, a mate, with green paroquets in a wooden cage. Here you will see sitting on a bench a sorrowful-looking woman, with new bright cooking tins at her feet, telling you she is an emigrant preparing for her voyage. As you pass along the quay the air is pungent with tobacco; on that it overpowers you with the fumes of rum; then you are nearly sickened with the stench of hides, and huge bins of horns; and shortly afterwards the

Above: The Govan-built RMS *Campania* at Liverpool Landing Stage. At 12,950 GRT, she was, at the time she entered service in 1893, the world's largest ship, and in 1893–4 she held the coveted Blue Riband.

Below left: Preston Docks, like those at Manchester, were inland and reached by navigating narrow inland waterways – in Preston's case, the River Ribble. The narrow lock-gated entrance to the docks restricted the size of vessels which could access the port.

Below: The 19,524-ton RMS *Caronia*, built for Cunard by John Brown on the Clyde in 1904.

atmosphere is fragrant with coffee and spice. Nearly everywhere you meet stacks of cork, or else yellow bins of sulphur, or lead-coloured copper ore. As you enter this warehouse, the floor is sticky, as if it had been newly tarred, with the sugar that has leaked through the casks.

The bustle of Victorian and Edwardian docks was as much about the people as it was about the ships. Thousands of men worked on the docks, and the increasing size of passenger liners meant ever more people were arriving and leaving Britain through the great ports of Southampton, Glasgow, London and Liverpool. Just as many were travelling through the country's many smaller ports like Falmouth, Hull, Cardiff, Bristol and Leith.

The ocean crossing they endured must have been difficult – in the mid-1800s, the average size of a transatlantic boat was considerably below 1,000 tons, and even at the dawn of the twentieth century, the gross tonnage of the largest passenger liner in the world – in 1905 that was the SS *Amerika* – had risen to only 22,000 tons. The average size of vessels serving routes to the Americas and to the outposts of empire was around 6,000 tons. What might be considered large ships in Edwardian times – relatively small by today's standards – were the exception. The Cunard steamer RMS *Caronia,* launched in 1904, had a gross tonnage of only 19,524. SS *Amerika* eclipsed her by 2,500 tons in the following year, but even *Amerika* would have a short stay in the record books – the 31,550-ton RMS *Lusitania* made her maiden voyage in 1907.

Barry Docks, *c.* 1904 – a mixture of sail and steam ships line the quaysides. The busy port handled everything from coastal tramp steamers and passenger ferries to large cargo ships. Many of the sailing ships were probably engaged in the trade between Barry and ports on Ireland's east coast, while the coal staithes at the right of the picture were used to export the produce from the Welsh coalfields.

A cargo steamer enters the lock at the entrance to Ipswich Docks, c. 1905. The docks had been dug in the 1840s, bringing iron ore and coal to the town, and exporting manufactured goods.

She could carry 2,198 passengers, and a crew of 850, and could cross the Atlantic at 25 knots, a phenomenal speed for the day.

The majority of cargo vessels, however, were anything but large. It is worth remembering that the Manchester Ship Canal, completed in 1894, and able to cope with the very largest cargo steamers of the day when it was opened, only ever managed to cope with vessels up to 12,000 tons before the introduction of containers and ever-larger vessels brought about its demise in the late 1970s.

Although we think of liners today as luxurious passenger ships, most Edwardian lines also carried cargo – and many depended on the Royal Mail for a key component of their income. Designated mail-carriers were styled 'RMS' rather than 'SS', and were an essential link with the Empire. The Royal Mail Steam Packet Company (RMSPCo) could trace its origins back to the earliest years of Victoria's reign when, in 1841, it acquired the contract to carry mail from Falmouth to the West Indies. It continued to operate that service for eighty years. By the 1850s the RMSPCo was also running weekly services to Lisbon, Brazil, Uruguay and Argentina and it was for that route that it commissioned the RMS *Araguaya* from Workman Clark's Yard in Belfast.

While the passengers only ever saw the smartly dressed officers and cabin crew, below decks a veritable army of stokers and boilermen was needed to keep these behemoths on the move. The twin-screw RMS *Carmania*, for example, had twelve double-ended Scotch boilers heated by 102 furnaces, with stokers shovelling coal into each furnace around the clock as long as the ship was steaming. In addition

To keep the passengers amused, several Edwardian shipping lines employed troupes of pierrots, offering the same mixture of entertainment found on many British beaches at the time.

The beautiful 10,537-ton RMS *Araguaya*, was the first of several large liners built for the Royal Mail Steam Packet Company during the Edwardian years. Her classic lines are evocative of the age. Uniquely for that period she was the only RMSPCo ship not ordered from Belfast's Harland & Wolff. She came, instead, from Workman Clark, and entered service to Brazil, Uruguay and Argentina in 1906.

Ayr, still one of Scotland's successful small ports today, had a busy harbour lining both sides of the River Ayr for centuries before the docks were extended and deepened in the nineteenth century. Hitherto limited by considerable rise and fall of the tide, the new enclosed dock greatly enhanced the port's attraction. By the end of the Edwardian era it was importing timber and a range of other goods, and shipping out huge tonnages of coal from the Ayrshire coalfields.

to the stokers, there were boilermen and engineers maintaining the engines so, despite the fact that there could be up to 2,000 passengers to take care of – 600 first class, 400 second class and 1,000 third class – quite a large number of her 424-man crew was employed well below the passenger decks just keeping the liner on the move. And keeping the liner at sea required prodigious amounts of coal, much of which was hand-loaded by labourers, many of them women in some of the smaller overseas ports.

When the First World War started in 1914, the Admiralty requisitioned many of Britain's passenger ships – from coastal paddle steamers to great liners. The RMS *Campania* was saved from being broken up, and became HMS *Campania*. She was converted into an early armoured aircraft carrier, her appearance radically changed in the process. She survived all but the last six days of the war; on 5 November 1918, after a series of collisions with two other warships – HMS *Royal Oak* and HMS *Glorious* – during high winds in the Firth of Forth, she sank.

COASTAL AND INLAND STEAMERS

The steamship was not a Victorian invention – the world's first steamboat, William Symington's, first sailed on the River Carron near Grangemouth in 1801, demonstrating the practicality of steam propulsion. Henry Bell's passenger-carrying paddle-steamer was launched on the Clyde in the closing weeks of 1811, and first sailed on 12 January 1812, a quarter of a century before Queen Victoria came to the throne. Mr Bell saw the steamer service as another means of bringing visitors to the Helensburgh Hotel which he ran with his wife. He cannot have envisaged the revolution he had started.

It was undoubtedly during the Victorian decades that the steamship's ascendancy and universal dominance revolutionised sea travel and cargo transport. It was, arguably, the steamship which drove the nineteenth century's huge expansion in world trade, held the British Empire together, and considerably eased transportation around the thousands of miles of coast which make up the British Isles. In remote areas where good roads had not yet been built, the regular steamers – taking over from sailing ships – were essential links with the rest of the country. It was often much easier to transport goods by sea than by land, and in Scotland, Wales and the Bristol Channel, steamer services developed quickly. In all probability, no Victorian

Opposite top: Passengers await the departure to Belfast of the turbine steamer SS *Londonderry* at Heysham, c. 1905. If the cranes look remarkably clean, that was because the port of Heysham had opened only in the previous year. She was built for the Midland Railway to serve their Belfast Express service, which left London, at about 5 p.m., and ran 270 miles from St Pancras to Heysham, where the steamer was waiting to transport passengers on to Belfast, delivering them there about 6.30 the next morning.

Above: The 271-ton paddle-steamer PS *Stirling Castle* makes her way along the River Forth from Stirling towards Alloa in 1904. Several small steamers plied the river between Leith or Granton and Alloa at that time. PS *Stirling Castle* served the route between 1899 and May 1907, when she was moved to the south coast. She needed telescopic funnels to get under the bridges in the upper river.

Opposite: Passengers disembark from the paddle-steamer *Princess May* at Ardlui Pier on Loch Lomond, 1907. The 256-ton steamer sailed the loch from 1898 until replaced by PS *Maid of the Loch* in 1953.

or Edwardian traveller ever undertook a complete circumnavigation of Britain's working coast. But once the steamer networks were fully established, it would have been possible!

By the closing years of the nineteenth century, nearly eighty seaside resorts had built piers. While most of them were developed into multi-purpose leisure facilities, almost all of those constructed before 1875 were conceived as landing stages for steamers. The pier offered a secure mooring at all stages of the tide, and some, like Southend, were extended on several occasions as the coastal strip silted up, thus ensuring that boats could still access them safely. Southend Pier eventually boasted a total length of over 6,600 feet. Many became so long that they needed railways to carry passengers from the pierhead to the land! For most of the piers constructed

in the closing three decades of the century, their role as landing stage was definitely secondary to their role as tourist attractions. Many did, however, continue to be served by regular steamer traffic until the early years of the twentieth century. Add to that the many hundreds of harbours, jetties and docks, and it is clear that in the days before railways became the dominant mode of transport, the coastal transport network was extensive indeed. Even after the railways became well established, steamers remained a popular and reliable form of coastal transport.

Starting in London, our late-Victorian traveller could have taken a steamer operated by any one of several companies from either London's Tower Bridge or Woolwich to Southend-on-Sea, onwards to Clacton-on-Sea, Harwich and Felixstowe. Services were extended to Southwold by 1890, and to Lowestoft and Great Yarmouth in the following year, operated by the General Steam Navigation Company. The route to Clacton was served by the London Woolwich and Clacton-on-Sea Steamship Company from 1890, and Belle Steamers ran to Great Yarmouth from 1897. Boats from London and Great Yarmouth passed at Walton on the Naze, where day trip passengers could change ships for the return journey.

In August 1888, the steam tug was involved in an incident near Cromer. This was before Cromer had a pier – the pier was completed in 1901 – and passengers had just embarked from the beach when the steamer struck the submerged church tower of the lost village of Shipden, which had lain beneath the water for five hundred years, and sank.

Left: The steamer *Rob Roy* pulls away from Trossachs Pier on Loch Katrine in 1897, taking visitors for a sail to Stronachlachar. She completed this journey at least once a day – except Sundays and Christmas – from her launch on the loch in 1856 until she was withdrawn from service in 1902.

Below: 'Perfectly reflected in the still waters, the steamer *Rob Roy* leaves Trossachs Pier for a sail on Loch Katrine, one of Scotland's most enduringly popular tourist sailings' This card was produced in the 1890s, just a few years before the present steamer, *Sir Walter Scott*, was introduced on to the loch.

The 996-ton paddle-steamer *Duchess of York* was built at R. & H. Green's yard in Blackwall, London, in 1895 for the South Eastern Railway's French service, but she had a very short life, being scrapped in 1904. The dredging of Dover harbour in the early 1900s rendered her redundant very quickly, as the railway companies found it more economical to run much larger screw-driven turbine steamers out of the newly deepened port.

Opposite page: The Caledonian Steam Packet Company's PS *Galatea* built in 1889, cruising on the Clyde, c. 1904.

Steamers left Skegness daily for Hunstanton, leaving at 8.30 a.m. and arriving off Hunstanton two-and-a-half hours later. The return journey northwards left Hunstanton at 5.30 p.m., arriving in Skegness by 8.00 p.m. The return fare at the close of the nineteenth century was 3s 0d. At the end of the tourist season, steamers which had spent the summer at Skegness returned to their home ports of Grimsby or Hull. Other Hull vessels worked the summer season elsewhere, such as the steam tug *Frenchman*, a familiar sight around Bridlington, from where it operated summer services up and down the Yorkshire coast. In addition to *Frenchman*, Bridlington was regularly visited by four other vessels in the 1890s and early 1900s: PS *General Havelock*, PS *Esme*, PS *Friends* and the largest, PS *Scarborough*.

The steamer *Dundee*, owned by the Dundee Perth & London Shipping Company, sailed directly from London's Dundee Wharf in Limehouse to Dundee Docks. Built in 1886, she was equipped with luxury cabins for sixty-five first-class passengers, cabins for sixty second-class passengers, and deck space for up to seventy-five third- or 'deck'- class travellers. The company also offered an overnight service between Hull and Dundee for many years. The port of Dundee was perfectly positioned to exploit the Fife coalfields, and the company had its own coal ship, which regularly crossed the Tay from Tayport loaded with Fife coal to fuel the steamers.

The Aberdeen Steam Navigation Company operated passenger and freight services between Aberdeen and London from as early as 1828. They also ran regular coastal services linking Aberdeen with Leith and Dundee.

Passenger services operated around Scotland's north-east coast from as early as the 1820s. In August 1826, the newspaper *Inverness Courier* carried an account of the first passenger steamship sailing round the north of Scotland by a tiny steamer, the

SS *United Kingdom* – which sailed from Glasgow, through the Hebrides, round Cape Wrath, up to Orkney, south again to Wick, Aberdeen and Newhaven on the Firth of Forth. Several sightings of early steamships belching smoke as they made their way slowly along the north-west coast of Scotland were reported at the time as being 'ships on fire'!

A regular service from Aberdeen to Wick and up to Stromness in the Orkneys was initiated just seven years later in 1833, and coastal steamers carrying both cargo and passengers – although only for those not in any sort of a hurry – plied between Aberdeen and Glasgow from the 1840s. From Glasgow or Ardrossan, there was a variety of services south to Fleetwood and Liverpool, calling at ports in south-west Scotland, Cumberland, Westmorland and Lancashire along the way.

From Liverpool there were regular steamer services to many of the holiday towns along the coast of North Wales during the summer months, and to some of the larger towns throughout the year. The Liverpool & North Wales Steamship Company Ltd operated services as far as Beaumaris by the 1880s, while the Dublin General Steamship Company offered passenger services on small paddle-steamers from Liverpool direct to Cardiff from the 1860s; for any traveller who needed a faster service, the Glasgow and Belfast Steam Packet Company ran a direct service from Glasgow to Cardiff from around 1870.

From Cardiff and Newport, a number of companies operated passenger boats and excursions across the Bristol Channel, to Bristol, Weston-super-Mare, Watchet, Minehead, Ilfracombe, Burnham on Sea, and elsewhere. From Bristol regular sailings connected Weston, Watchet and Minehead to North Devon and Cornwall. From Penzance, Bazeleys started regular services to London in the 1840s, sometimes

David MacBrayne's steamship PS *Pioneer* at the jetty at Corpach in 1903. This was a 'classic' view of the jetty with the mountains towering above it, and was used by many photographers and postcard publishers. The company founded by David MacBrayne still serves Scotland's west coast today as Caledonian MacBrayne.

carrying passengers, and other operators ran direct services from Torquay to London.

From Weymouth, excursion steamers regularly ferried tourists to Lulworth Cove – where they had to 'walk the plank' from the bows of the ship down on to the beach – and there were also regular services to Bournemouth and Poole, and to Portsmouth. Several steamship owners ran competing summer excursion services connecting Bournemouth to London. The Brighton, Worthing & South Coast Steamboat Company, later bought by P & A Campbell, operated regular steamers from Brighton to Boulogne in France. More local services sailed to the Isle of Wight, to Worthing, and to Newhaven, Seaford, Eastbourne and Hastings. Campbell's steamer, the *Albion*, registered in Bristol, set the record – never since beaten – for completing the fastest trip between Brighton and Eastbourne in only one hour and six minutes! The single fare for the journey in 1909 was 1s 6d.

The popularity of the steamer services along the south-east coast at the end of the nineteenth century should not be underestimated. Steamers used Hastings Pier so frequently in the second half of the century that an additional landing stage was added in 1885 allowing three steamers to tie up at any one time. Services operated by the Hastings St Leonards & Eastbourne Steamboat Company on their steamers PS *Seagull* and PS *Britannia* ran regularly to destinations between Eastbourne and Dover throughout late Victorian and Edwardian summers. From Eastbourne, there were also summer excursions as far as Ramsgate and Margate. Our traveller could have boarded the paddle steamer *Golden Eagle*, or the turbine screw steamer *Kingfisher* or, for a time, the PS *Royal Sovereign* for the journey from Ramsgate, via Margate, to London Bridge.

The PS *Brodick Castle*, bought by Richard Cosens in 1902, is seen here leaving Bournemouth Pier in 1908 on her way to Swanage. Two year larter, stripped of her fittings, she sank on tow in 1910 off Portland Bill. At high tide passengers could embark from the side of the pier as well as from the pierhead – saving them much of the 1,000-foot walk from dry land.

Above: The PS *Prince of Wales* was built in 1887 by Fairfield Engineering on the Clyde, for the Isle of Man, Liverpool and Manchester Steamship Co Ltd (Manx Line), and worked the crossing between Liverpool and Douglas until 1915 when she was sold to the Admiralty. She was over 340 feet long and had a 40-foot beam and a gross tonnage of 1,547 tons. Her two steam engines developed 6,500 horsepower, giving her a top speed of 23 knots. She is seen here at Liverpool's famous Landing Stage.

Left: David MacBrayne's 1891-built steamer *Lord of the Isles* disembarking a large complement of passengers at Inveraray Pier in the 1890s. The photograph was published as a tinted postcard by James Valentine in the early 1900s. The name *Lord of the Isles* is still used by Caledonian MacBrayne today.

Below: The 283-ton PS *Brodick Castle* was built in Paisley in 1878 by H. McIntyre & Co, originally intended to serve the Isle of Arran, but she stayed only nine years in Scottish waters before moving to the south coast where she worked until 1910. This photograph dates from the 1880s.

A horse and handler make their way along the towpath on the Cromford Canal at Whatstandwell in Derbyshire. The 14-mile Cromford Canal opened in 1794 and was effectively abandoned in 1962.

All dressed up for a works, church or club outing along the Leeds Liverpool Canal, around 1908–10.

ON INLAND WATERWAYS

Although Britain's canal network was largely the creation of the eighteenth century, inland waterways were still key components of the national transport network well into the twentieth. Some saw the development of the railways in the first half of the nineteenth century as the death-knell of the canals but, with so many mills and factories built alongside canal towpaths, their continued success was in no immediate danger from the train. Indeed, it was well towards the close of the nineteenth century before many new industrial developments eschewed the canal and developed railway access for their raw materials and completed goods.

The canals were major employers, and huge fleets of barges plied the canals carrying everything from heavy loads of coal to lighter cargoes of mixed goods. It was only when the scale of manufacturing expanded and the expected speed of delivery shortened in the second half of the nineteenth century that the logistics of canal transport started to be questioned. Even so, carriage by canal, albeit slow, was relatively cheap, and for many non-urgent goods represented excellent value for money. After decades of neglect, the attraction of canal and river transport is now on the rise, with several large companies exploring the 'green' benefits of the barge.

Barges making their way across the Barton Aqueduct over the Manchester Ship Canal. The aqueduct carried narrowboats on the Bridgewater Canal over the lowered masts and funnels of the ocean-going liners and cargo vessels which used the Ship Canal. The Bridgewater Canal, opened in 1761, was the first canal in England to be cut along a completely new route, independent of existing rivers and lakes.

Left: Thames boatmen, photographed by John Thomson in the 1870s. Thomson titled this image 'On the Silent Highway', and it appeared as a plate in his 1878 publication *Street Life in London*.

Above: A small boy watches a steam barge approach Lock 16 on the Forth & Clyde Canal, c. 1907.

Below: Passengers relax on a horse-drawn pleasure craft on the Llangollen Canal, c. 1905, while the horse is given a well-earned rest and a chance to graze for a few moments.

Judging by this 1904 postcard, the ferryman at Cramond, Edinburgh, could carry fourteen passengers.

The Renfrew Ferry crossed the Clyde between Renfrew and Yoker, and the chain ferry seen here was brought into service in 1897. It could carry passengers and a small number of wagons. The service continued to carry both passengers and vehicles until 1984. Today's ferries are for passengers only.

ON THE FERRIES

In the days before motor transport, with much lighter traffic on the roads, there were many fewer bridges, so the ferry was a vital link in the transport network. Ferries ranged from small open rowing boats across narrow rivers, to quite large, vehicle-carrying vessels on the major estuaries.

Steam power heralded a new era for the chain ferry where the boat hauled itself across the river using a fixed cable or chain. This was a highly effective means of working, removing the need to steer the boat in strong river currents. Before steam, these boats were rope hauled by nothing more than man-power. In the Victorian and Edwardian eras, they proved popular subjects for both photographers and postcard publishers.

In the 1860s there were hundreds of small boats criss-crossing the River Thames, as well as some larger ferries. While most of the five hundred licensed – and innumerable unlicensed – boats were really no more than water taxis, some could carry more than twenty people. By then there were over a hundred passenger steamers working the river as well. Henry Mayhew, writing in 1861, noted that the first steam ferry on the Thames, the *Margery*, carried her first fare-paying passengers in 1818, only six years after Henry Bell's *Comet* first sailed on the Clyde. Unusually, *Margery* was a stern-wheeler. The Woolwich Ferry, which can trace its origins back to the early fourteenth century, did not embrace steam power until 1888, when the paddlers *Duncan*, *Gordon* and *Hutton* were brought into service. These ships were licensed to carry up to a thousand passengers and up to twenty carriages and carts.

A chain ferry operated across the River Blyth in Northumberland for many years, with a steam service introduced in the late nineteenth century. After 130 years, the service was withdrawn, but plans are in hand which seek to reintroduce a ferry across the river. The ferry is typical of the design adopted by many river services, and used a very simple vertical domed boiler to power the steam engine. Larger boats in Southampton, Barrow, and elsewhere, could cater for more vehicles.

Above: The Windermere Ferry on its way across the lake with the Furness Abbey coach on board. Just behind the horses we can see the simple vertical boiler connected to the steam engine which pulled the vessel along the chain.

Above right: The Ferry, Stockton, 1903. A fleet of large rowing boats worked ferrying workers across the busy River Tees. The boat in the centre of the picture has at least twenty-six passengers!

Below: A busy scene on the slipway at what was probably the biggest floating bridge of the Edwardian era – the massive Woolston Ferry. It crossed the River Itchen at Southampton, and formed a key part of the route between that city and Portsmouth. The ferry was not replaced by a bridge until 1977, and before then, thirteen different vessels had operated the chain-ferry service. The last was numbered '14' to avoid bad luck! The first ferry opened in 1836 between Southampton and Itchen Ferry, and a second set of chains was laid in 1881 to enable traffic capacity to be doubled. The ferries took four minutes to make the crossing, at a speed of 100 metres per minute.

Above: Ocean Road, South Shields. As a reminder of the fact that the postcard was the everyday form of communication, with several deliveries each day, 'M' wrote to Mr J. Howard on this card in July 1908, 'If you can possibly come up tonight do so, as I wants to see you very particular'.

Below: The Stirling & Bridge of Allan Tramways Company operated both single and double-decker vehicles along this route. They had introduced horse-drawn trams in 1874 and continued with a horse-drawn service until 1920. Stirling never electrified its system, preferring instead to rip up the lines and introduce motor buses along the former tram routes.

Above right: St Augustine's Bridge and the Tramway Centre, Bristol, 1904. After twenty years of operating horse-drawn trams, Bristol became the first city in Britain to introduce electric vehicles in 1895.

DING-DING WENT THE TRAM

The credit for being Britain's first tramline is usually given to the Swansea & Mumbles Railway which started operating horse-drawn cars on rails as early as 1807. The advantage of the tram was that with reduced friction from the wheels, on rails rather than cobbles, a single horse could pull a much greater load, and the passengers would enjoy a much smoother ride. Horse-drawn tramways were developed all over Britain in the second half of the nineteenth century, first as single-decked vehicles, and later as two-horse double-deckers.

Two major improvements to tramways came in the 1870s: steam-hauled vehicles, and cable-hauled systems. Steam tram engines proved very popular in England, with several towns and cities adopting them, and companies like Kitson of Leeds exported their steam technology all over the world. The steam tractor unit was powerful enough to pull two tramcars, so at busy times of the day these vehicles really came into their own.

The world's first cable-hauled tramway opened on Highgate Hill in London in 1891, followed shortly afterwards by another line in Brixton, but they did not last long. Although cable-hauled trams became popular in America, New Zealand and elsewhere, they were slow to catch on in Britain, but in 1899, with the opening of the Edinburgh cable tramway, all that changed. Over the next twenty years,

Keeping a safe distance from the horse-drawn cab in front, and with not a motor car in sight, tramcar No 644 – introduced in 1901 – makes its way along Sauchiehall Street in Glasgow around 1905. The clock on the building in the middle distance, showing five past eight, identifies this scene as the beginning of the morning rush hour, yet the upper decks of the trams seem remarkably empty.

Left: Liverpool tram No 159 makes its way along Church Street, c. 1905. This design of electric car, built by Dick, Kerr, first appeared on Liverpool's streets in 1900, and some of the vehicles were operated for more than thirty years.

Below left: Tramcars on Aberdeen's Union Street, c. 1910. Car No 16 had been built as an open-topped vehicle, and was the only vehicle in the fleet fitted with this experimental top deck roof. It reportedly made the vehicle top heavy!

Above: A single-deck tram sits outside Coventry station, c .1905. The town's first tramline opened in 1884 and ran from the station to Bedworth. The 3'6"-gauge open-topped cars were steam-hauled until the system was electrified in 1895. Parts of Coventry's extensive tram system survived until the infamous German bombing on the night of 14 November 1940 destroyed much of the network.

the city's system developed into the most extensive cable tramway in the world. Edinburgh had kept horse-drawn trams long after most cities had electrified, and so ideally suited was the cable system to the city's hilly terrain that electric trams did not appear until the 1920s.

Tram systems were developed by a surprisingly large number of British towns and cities – the construction of new lines being approached with the same sort of evangelical zeal which had accompanied railway-building decades earlier.

London's first experimental horse-drawn tram appeared as early as 1860, the first line being operated by the delightfully named George Train. The experiment was not a success, as the tramlines were laid on top of the cobbles and thus disrupted all the other traffic! Trams using recessed rails first appeared in the early 1870s, and by the mid-1870s, some operators were already experimenting with steam-powered cars.

By the late 1880s, London already had an extensive system, with trams operated by several different companies. The largest of these, the North Metropolitan Tramways

Three different transport systems in one picture – a motor car, one of Edinburgh's cable-hauled trams (behind the car), and an electric Musselburgh tram – photographed in 1905 where the two tramways met at Joppa.

Officials from Wigan Corporation Tramways stand in front of car No 45 – built by Hurst Nelson of Motherwell – after a test run on the extension of the route to Orrell in April 1906.

A tram on the Pierhead service in South Shields, parked near the Wouldrave Memorial, *c.* 1906. South Shields withdrew the last of its trams from service in 1946.

Company, later known as the North London Tramways Company, had a large fleet of steam powered units built by Dick, Kerr & Company, but while passengers liked them, pedestrians and residents were less impressed by the smoke and the noise. Most of London's steam trams at that time, however, served the suburbs, with horse-drawn omnibuses connecting with the cars at Blackfriars, Vauxhall, and London bridges to take passengers into the city.

Tramlines were never laid within the City of London, or in the West End, but despite that, London's network was the biggest in the world by the end of the Edwardian era.

Over a hundred towns and cities laid tramlines, many originally built by private companies, but all eventually owned and operated by the local corporations and town and city councils.

In the days before motor cars, trams were an ideal solution to the movement of large numbers of people, but when motor transport started to appear on the streets, the trams and their lines became a traffic hazard. Many towns and cities had abandoned their trams before the Second World War, in favour of buses or trolley buses, and by the 1950s, all had gone. It is ironic that trams are being reintroduced in an attempt to reduce the impact of the motor cars which originally brought about their withdrawal from service.

This remarkable picture of the Camborne & Redruth Tramway's industrial line shows tin stone being transported by tram from East Pool tin mine near Redruth, some time before 1910. On the back of the card, a wealth of detail has been written in – the splendidly uniformed driver was Mr J. Williams, and his brakeman Bill Hampton. At the rear of the trio on the locomotive stands Fred Myners who, according to the pencilled notes, 'was brought home by tram/hearse on his death'.

The 3'6" narrow gauge Camborne & Redruth Tramway gave the construction of its 3.4-mile track to

Dick, Kerr & Co., who had a long and successful record of developing tramways and locomotives – especially steam traction units for early urban tram networks. They had manufacturing facilities in Kilmarnock and Preston. Perhaps surprisingly, given that Dick, Kerr & Co had laid out the system, all the tramway's electric vehicles were manufactured by G. F. Milnes of Hadley in Shropshire. The line opened to passengers in November 1902, with the mineral traffic operating via two small branch lines from May of the following year. Passenger services survived until 1927; mineral traffic until 1934.

HAILING A CAB

The first licensed horse-drawn cabs appeared on London's streets in 1823, and the first hansom cab took to the road just before Victoria came to the throne. For sixty years they had little competition, until the first battery-powered electric 'horseless carriages' appeared in 1897. And in 1898 they were joined by the first licensed petrol-driven cab, but these did not become popular until after 1903.

Throughout the nineteenth century, the two-wheeled 'hansom' and the four-wheeled 'growler' were the mainstays of the licensed cab trade, and variations of the design of the hansom were to be found all over the world.

The costs of cab hire in London were sometimes difficult to fathom: despite Charles Dickens Jnr's advice to his readers that they were simple, it took him nearly a page of his 1888 *Dictionary of London* to explain them! Fares were tightly controlled within a 4-mile radius of Charing Cross, but travel a few yards outside that circle and, unless prior agreement on the fare had been reached with the driver, he seems to have been at liberty to charge very much higher rates. The passenger could hire the cab or carriage by distance or by time – but the maximum distance which could be agreed was 6 miles, and the maximum duration of any hire was limited to one hour. Thereafter the price had to be re-negotiated. In 1887, the fare for a 2-mile

Left: Electric trams and four-wheeled carriages await passengers outside Newcastle Central Station, c. 1902. The four-wheel 'Growler' was based on the design of the brougham.

Below left: A pair of cabs waiting for passengers outside Wimbledon Station in the summer of 1906.

Below: A beautifully tinted A & G Taylor postcard, c. 1903, shows the classic lines of the lightweight hansom cab waiting with its driver just off the Strand in the City of London.

The cab rank in the High Street, Dumfries, c. 1906. A quartet of four-wheeled 'growlers' await hire, while their drivers pass the time in idle chat. All Dumfries cabs at this time were four-seat carriages.

A Scarborough Jockey Carriage, 1904. Professional jockeys earned extra money manning these very exclusive unlicensed carriages. With the driver astride the horse rather than seated on the carriage, the occupants were afforded rather more privacy for their intimate journey together!

Although this postcard is entitled 'London Electric Cab', it is actually a Beeston Humber of about 1904–5, possibly a 10–12 hp model. The lady peering out of the back is Miss Madge Crichton, a well-known actress and singer of the period.

journey from Charing Cross was 1s, and 6d a mile (or part of a mile) thereafter – in real terms much more expensive than today!

Cab stands were regulated by the Metropolitan Police from the early 1840s, and they also regulated and inspected both the cabs and the cabmen's shelters. In the 1880s most cab stands were manned from 10 a.m. until 10 p.m., but Charing Cross, at the heart of the system, was manned for 24 hours a day, as were the stands in the Strand, Kensington and Pall Mall, and the stand outside the Houses of Parliament when the house was in session.

Perhaps understandably, horse-cabs survived a lot longer in the provinces than they did in London. In provincial cities, they survived through much of the Edwardian era, and in some places until the outbreak of the Great War.

Bersey's electric carriage – known as the 'humming bird' on account of the unusual sound of its motor and introduced by the London Electric Cab Company – enjoyed a brief period of popularity, but it did not last beyond the introduction of petrol-driven taxicabs. Records show that in 1905 there were fewer than twenty motor taxis in the whole of London. A year later there were almost one hundred.

When the General Motor Cab Company imported five hundred Renault cabs in the following year, the motor taxicab rapidly became the norm rather than the exception. As early French cars were right-hand drive – the driver sat at the pavement side of the vehicle in order to quickly open doors for his passengers – they were already suited to British roads. By 1910, the number of licences issued for motor taxis exceeded horse-cab licences for the first time.

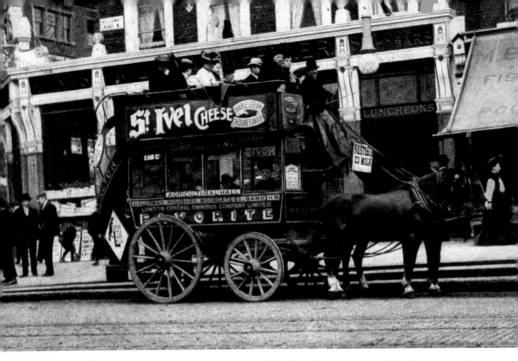

The strength of the horses pulling these wooden-bodied omnibuses over the cobbled streets must have been immense. They could seat at least fifteen people on the upper deck and thirteen on the lower deck, together with however many standing passengers might be squeezed in! Even in 1904–5 when these photographs were taken, the importance of the bus as a moving advertising hoarding had clearly been recognised, with every bus festooned with advertisements for sweets, tobacco, coffee and, of course, that Victorian panacea for all ills, Carter's Little Liver Pills.

ON THE BUSES

As Charles Dickens Jnr writes in his *Dictionary of London 1888, An Unconventional Handbook*:

> The omnibus service of London is chiefly in the hands of the London General
> Omnibus Company (Limited), whose carriages traverse the leading thoroughfares
> in every direction at regular intervals from early morning to midnight. Besides the
> company there are also on the principle routes one or two large private proprietors,
> and a considerable number of smaller owners, who run their vehicles more or less at
> discretion, as well as lines between the great railway stations.

There is a sense that Dickens liked to encourage competition, for he continues:

> The London General Omnibus Company has lately met with fresh competition in the
> London Road Car Company (Limited), which has offices at 9, Grosvenor-rd, Westminster,
> and at the present time has convenient vehicles running on the following five lines: Victoria
> Stn., *viâ* Charing +, Fleet-st, and Bank, to Broad-st Stn., every 8 min. Hammersmith-
> broadway, *viâ* Piccadilly, Strand, etc., to Liverpool-st and London-br. Waltham-gn, *viâ*
> Fulham-rd and Piccadilly to London-br. Waltham-gn, *viâ* King's-rd Sloane-sq, Victoria, and
> Strand to Liverpool-st.

Then, over more than ten pages, the London General's bus timetable is published, and judging by the number of routes and the frequency of the services thereon, the bus companies between them must have had several thousand horses.

The old meets the new – passengers boarding a horse-drawn omnibus in Birmingham, c. 1905, while others watch from the open top back of a passing motor bus on its way to Birmingham's New Street Station. Motor buses could carry more passengers more quickly, and after the purchase cost of the motor vehicle had been paid, they could be operated more cheaply. But the motor bus put many people out of work and, of course, required the driver to acquire a completely new set of skills.

Many of the London General buses were styled 'Favorite' on their sides, and as early as the 1880s, a colour coding for each route had come into being. So Dickens lists the vehicle colours and styling, as well as giving the details of the frequency and the fares on each of the 175 services listed. (Interestingly, more than a quarter of a century earlier in 1861, their buses had been styled 'favourite', rather than what today would be considered an American spelling.) The company had been set up in 1856, and continued to operate buses until 1933.

In the chapter on London Omnibuses in Volume III of his 1861 *London Labour and the London Poor*, Henry Mayhew lists many of the smaller private operators as well as the larger companies, and offers an estimation of the scale of the omnibus network. And when one places his comments in the context of the number of people moved around London today by bus, tube and train, the development of the city and the increased mobility of people over the past 150 years is there for all to see.

He writes:

> The total number of omnibuses traversing the streets of London is about 3000. The
> number of conductors and drivers is about 7000. The receipts of each vehicle vary

Left: 'Cast-iron Billy', William Parragreen, was photographed in 1876 or 1877 by John Thomson for his book *Street Life in London*. Billy had been an omnibus driver 'forty-three years on the road or more' until rheumatism forced his retirement.

The London General Omnibus Company Limited was quick to recognise the importance of branding and brand recognition. With picture postcards the most common and convenient method by which people kept in touch, they exploited the medium by producing beautifully tinted photographs of their vehicles. 'This is something new in postcards,' wrote W. M. B. to Miss Eva Lea in Bristol in February 1905. But by the time these remarkable cards were marketed, the days of the horse-drawn bus were drawing to a close. Just a few weeks after this card was posted, London's first motor bus appeared.

Above: An early De Dion Bouton motor bus makes its way along Hagley Road, Birmingham, in 1906.

from 2*l*. to 4*l*. per day. Estimating the whole 3000 at 3*l*., it follows that the entire sum expended annually in omnibus hire by the people of London amounts to no less than 3,285,000*l*., which is more than 30*s*. a head for every man, woman, and child in the metropolis. The average journey as regards length of each omnibus is six miles, and that distance is in some cases travelled twelve times a-day by each omnibus, or, as it is called, 'six there and six back'. Some perform the journey only ten times a-day (each omnibus), and some, but a minority, a less number of times. Now taking the average as between forty-five and fifty miles a day travelled, and that I am assured by the best authority is within the mark … we find a travel as it was worded to me, upwards of 140,000 miles a-day, or a yearly travel of more than 50,000,000 miles: an extent that almost defies a parallel among any distances popularly familiar.

And that was just in London! By the 1880s, that figure had increased substantially, and by the early years of the twentieth century, it is said to have more than doubled.

Motor buses started to appear on British streets in 1905 when London General ordered its first fifty vehicles. Some were made by De Dion Bouton, others by Sidney Straker & Squire Limited, and within six years, the last of the horse-drawn vehicles had been withdrawn. Those first years, however, were marked by numerous accidents, as driver training was still largely a thing of the future! The second generation of London motor buses, built by LGOC to their own standard design, started to appear early in 1910. The advent of the motor bus also saw a step backwards in terms of passenger route identification – the colour-coding of omnibuses according to their route was abandoned, and all the company's new motor buses were painted red, a tradition which endures to this day.

T. Clark ran a regular bus service from the station in Seaton, Devon, to the Beach Hotel. In the summer of 1905, there was often more luggage than passengers!

A group of children watch a new road surface being laid along the waterfront outside the Starbank Arms in Trinity, Edinburgh, around 1908.

A steam tractor unit pulls a train of small tramcars along the front at Douglas, Isle of Man, in 1903.

STEAM ON THE ROADS

The importance of the steam engine in Victorian times cannot be over-estimated. Not only did it power the steamer, the trains and many of the trams, but it also powered the vehicles which were used to build Britain's expanding network of roads, and offered road builders a much faster and more effective way of compacting the road surface than any horse-drawn roller could ever have done. The massive weight of the steam road roller itself was the key to its effectiveness. Steam also powered a generation of cars and lorries.

There was much concern in government circles about the damage which the huge weight of steam-powered vehicles could do to the roads, but supporters of steam power argued that the weight distribution over several wheels meant they were actually less damaging than horses. Looking at the narrow, solid-tyred wheels on some steam lorries, this is hard to believe, especially when a fully laden vehicle like the one shown weighed well over 9 tons!

A steam carriage was one of the five exhibits at the first ever horseless carriage show at Tunbridge Wells in 1895, and Thornycroft exhibited both steam lorries and steam-powered street sweeping and washing vehicles at the Crystal Palace in 1903, while a dozen companies showed off their steam cars.

From the catalogue to the show, published by *Autocar*, comes a list of names – none of which survived more than a few years: Cockshoot & Co, The Clarkson & Capel

John Thornycroft & Co developed this articulated six-wheeled lorry powered by a compound horizontal steam engine in 1896 at their works in Basingstoke. The company then advertised itself as 'Engineers, Shipbuilders & Motor Manufacturers'. With a load area on its platform of 110 square feet, it could carry five tons at a stately 5 mph. The vehicle itself, fully fuelled up and in steam, weighed in at 4 tons 5 cwt!

An Aveling & Porter steamroller, with caravan and trailer, parked near roadworks at Fareham Creek, Portsmouth, c. 1904. The company had produced their first steamroller as early as 1865.

A Foden Excelsior steam wagon and trailer in service with a Wigan removals firm, c. 1909 or 1910. Fodens had started building steam lorries in 1902, continuing to build them into the 1930s.

De Dion Bouton's first steam-powered car was launched in 1883, and while it represented progress, it was not practical. The power from the steam engine drove the front wheels, while the car was steered using a tiller to turn the rear wheels. The prototype car did not survive a catastrophic fire. Their 1884 model steered with the front wheels, and was driven by the back wheels. Although they continued making steam vehicles until 1904, De Dion Bouton had turned to making petrol cars by the late 1880s.

Steam Car Syndicate, Gardner-Serpollet, the Hydroleum Motor Vapomobile, the New Automobile Co's Miesse Car, J. L. Sandy's New Saracen car, The Speedwell Motor Company, the Victoria Carriage Works' Toledo models, the Weston Steam Car, and White Steam Cars have all been consigned to an obscure corner of history. And yet, each of those companies had great hopes for their products. The Victoria Carriage Works showed four models of their American-built Toledos at the show, while Speedwell showed six, ranging in power from 6 hp to 40 hp. On Stand 162, the Weston Motor Syndicate exhibited several Weston Steam Cars, 'fitted with all the latest 1903 Weston improvements' according to their advertising, including the 'Touring Trap' (priced at £260), the 'Touring Car' (£246), the 'Stanhope Runabout' (£211), the 'Indian Trap' with paraffin burner (£275) and the 'Victoria Modele de Luxe' (a hefty £255), so they were anything but cheap. Moreover, getting up steam with a paraffin burner cannot have been the speediest of exercises.

Steam cars did not sell well – the petrol engine was cleaner and much easier to operate – but despite public objection to their smoke and smell, steam lorries were sold widely, and their load-carrying ability helped them survive well into the 1930s.

BRIDGES BIG AND SMALL

The Victorian transport revolution led to bridge construction on a hitherto unprecedented scale. The building of the great railway bridges across the Forth, the Tay, the Tamar and elsewhere, was covered by some of the country's leading photographers – James Valentine and George Washington Wilson independently on the great Scottish bridges, and Roger Fenton on the building of Brunel's bridge over the Tamar. And once completed, all the country's major bridges continued to attract the attention of Victorian photographers and Edwardian postcard publishers.

One notable and truly unique bridge was the famous Crumlin Viaduct in South Wales, completed over half a century before the Forth was spanned. Opened in 1857 after four years of construction, the viaduct which carried the Newport, Hereford and Abergavenny Railway was hailed as one of the greatest achievements

Below: A rare carte-de-visite photograph of the Forth Bridge, photographed from North Queensferry, in the weeks just before it was completed in 1890. The spans are complete, but there are still cranes on the nearest tower, and over the first main span. Victorians flocked to watch progress on what was considered to be one of the marvels of the Victorian world, and photographs of the construction work were available in a variety of formats – large prints to be pasted into albums, stereo (3D) views, and cartes-de-visite to be slipped into the family album.

Right: A spectacular postcard of the Runcorn and Widnes Transporter Bridge laden with passengers. Judging by their dress, this was a special occasion, perhaps opening day in May 1905. The bridge was first contemplated in 1899, and took nearly five years to design and build. It should have been formally opened by King Edward VII, but he was ill on the great day. The first crossing over the Mersey at Runcorn Gap – previously either two ferries or a railway journey were needed – the bridge also spanned the Manchester Ship Canal. It proved expensive to build, and the anticipated income did not materialise as quickly as expected. The bridge company sold it to Runcorn Corporation in 1911 who operated it for fifty years before it was demolished and replaced by a road bridge in 1961.

THE FORTH BRIDGE. (FROM N.W.) EDINBURGH. Spans 1710 feet; Height above high water, 361 feet; Total length, 2766½ yards. THE PHOTOGLYPTIC CO.

Above: One of Belle Steamers' boats taking on passengers below London Bridge, c. 1908. The now-familiar shape of Tower Bridge can be seen beyond, completed fourteen years earlier in 1894.

Bottom: The crew of the Newport Transporter Bridge, c. 1910, just four years after the bridge over the River Usk was opened.

Right: The Runcorn and Widnes Transporter Bridge under construction in 1903. By then the 180-foot high towers were complete and work had just started on the 250-ton, 1,000-foot long steel girders from which the transporter car would be hung. The car carried 300 passengers more than 80 feet above the River Mersey and the Manchester Ship Canal.

of the Industrial Age. Towering high above the valley, its slender girders seemed altogether too light and delicate to carry trains. But it survived with surprisingly little modification or maintenance until closure and demolition in 1967.

Complex steelwork was also at the heart of Victorian London's most iconic bridge, although this was not immediately apparent. The 1884 design of Tower Bridge was necessary to permit increasingly large ships to pass through the bridge, which would cross the Thames at one of the busiest parts of the Port of London. The bridge may look as though it is stone-built, but at its core is a massive steel framework – 11,000 tons of it! It took a workforce of nearly five hundred people over eight years to build what was at the time the world's largest bascule bridge, and the roadway was raised and lowered using steam engines and sophisticated hydraulic pumps.

Edwardian Britain's three transporter bridges also depended on huge quantities of steel. Perhaps surprisingly, Britain built more of these strange structures than any other country. One such bridge had been built in the 1890s, and another two would follow in the reign of George V, but two were constructed between 1900 and 1906, over the Esk at Newport in South Wales and, the longest transporter span ever built in Britain, the Runcorn–Widnes Bridge in Cheshire.

The bustle of horse-drawn vehicles crossing London Bridge, as photographed, c. 1902. The bridge, which had been opened by King William IV in 1831, was claimed to be the busiest place in London at the dawn of the twentieth century, with over 9,000 people an hour using it – 8,000 pedestrians, and almost a thousand in buses, carriages and cabs. It was considerably widened between 1902 and 1904 to cope with increasing traffic, and sold to America in 1969.

Britain's fear of the horseless carriage led to some highly restrictive legislation which impeded the development of the motor car quite considerably. Many impediments were put in its path — such as the Victorian requirement that a red flag precede a motorised vehicle by day, and a red lantern by night — but after the repeal of the red flag law in 1896, the rise of the motor car was dramatic. Designs for steam-powered cars, coaches and omnibuses — many of them pre-dating Queen Victoria's accession to the throne — never got far beyond experimental stages, because they could not be used on most British roads. After 1896, however, development and innovation progressed at some pace, albeit a decade after the potential of the internal combustion engine had been proven. By the very early 1900s, names such as Royce, Thornycroft, Lanchester, Napier and others had already started to build petrol-driven motor vehicles.

Above: John Watts stands to the right of his fleet of cars outside Watts Yard Motor House and Repair Shop in Sinclair Street, Helensburgh, Strathclyde. He commissioned this postcard in 1904 and sent it to his customers as a promotional exercise in February 1905. Given the cost of a specially commissioned tinted postcard, he must have had a very successful business. Watts had already developed a wide range of motor services — the selling and repair of vehicles, and the provision of a fleet of chauffeur-driven cars available for hire by the more affluent visitors to the Firth of Clyde resort.

Left: Salisbury High Street already had a garage and Michelin tyre dealership by 1906.

CLINCHER

This remarkable 'cabinet' print dates from between 1896 and 1902, and offers a very rare view inside a motor vehicle repair workshop. Work is under way on two cars, a tricycle and a bicycle. To the left, one engineer seems to be working on a lathe of some sort, but research has so far failed to identify what the large castings on the floor might have been for. The 'Clincher' tyres, advertised on the wall, are the type of tyre common on today's bicycles, where air pressure alone holds the tyre in place on the rim. At the time this photograph was taken, pneumatic tyres with inner tubes were a relatively new innovation.

The location of the workshop is believed to be somewhere in Glasgow. Experts on early vehicles suggest that the motorised tricycle being worked on is a modified De Dion design, while the car is an early 10 hp Arrol-Johnston design from the late 1890s. The Mo-Car Syndicate Ltd was formed in late 1895 and started building Arrol-Johnston cars in the following year, using a part-wooden bodywork. The cars were designed by George Johnston and financed by William Arrol. Intriguingly, the large metal castings in the foreground are believed to be from a marine steam engine.

At Britain's first Automobile Show, organised by the new Society of Motor Manufacturers and Traders and held at the Crystal Palace in 1903, car names which are still familiar to us today made their first appearances. Cars from Daimler, Humber, Argyll, De Dion Bouton, Mercedes and many others drew the crowds. That year saw the first Vauxhalls, steered by a tiller rather than a wheel – their first model even featured passenger seats below and in front of the driver!

Autocar magazine, then in its eighth year of publication, produced a catalogue to accompany the show. In addition to the many petrol-driven models on show, and a range of steam-powered vehicles, the catalogue listed four electric carriages, two of which proudly proclaimed a range of 45–50 miles on a single battery charge. As history has proven, it took electric cars a very long time to get far beyond that! Describing one such electric carriage which had been sold to Queen Victoria, the exhibition catalogue proclaimed:

> We understand that Her Majesty is in the habit of driving the vehicle herself, and is delighted
> with the ease and simplicity of control and manipulation. The carriage was supplied to H.M.
> by the City and Suburban Electric Carriage Co, of 6, Denman Street, Piccadilly Circus, who
> also have a number of orders in hand from members of the nobility of both sexes.

By the time of the 1910 show, now known as the International Motor Exhibition and held at Earls Court, names like Ford had joined the ranks of car manufacturers, and a three-wheeled sports car, the Morgan, was seen in public for the first time.

A car makes its way along a Surrey lane near Epsom in 1908. Getting petrol then was still a challenge in parts of Britain, and motorists eagerly looked out for signs where they could buy cans of Pratt's Perfection Motor Spirit, PGR (Petroles de Grosnyi), Shell or other fuels. Oil companies were quick to advertise themselves in road atlases aimed primarily at drivers, which started to appear around 1905.

This is a detail from a postcard showing Drigg Vicarage in Cumberland, posted in 1906. The car, tiller-steered and rear-engined, is an 1896 model Arnold, based on a Benz design, and manufactured in Peckham for only two years between 1896 and 1898.

A motor car approaches the ford in Drumtochty Glen south of Banchory, Aberdeenshire, c. 1910.

The Royal Engineers preparing to launch one of their observational balloons at Long Valley, Aldershot in 1906. The army school of ballooning, established in Chatham in 1888, moved to Aldershot in 1890.

It is believed that this photograph of *Nulli Secundus* was taken after her enforced landing at Crystal Palace on the afternoon of 5 October 1907. A large crowd has gathered around the craft, some of them still holding the bicycles they used to get there. Five days later, some of her guy ropes broke free in the wind and, to avoid further damage, she was deflated, dismantled and returned to Farnborough.

TAKING TO THE AIR

When Colonel John Capper and Samuel Cody took to the air on 5 October 1907 at the controls of *Nulli Secundus*, Britain's first military aircraft, they cannot have imagined the importance that flight would have in both military activities and civil transport. *Nulli Secundus*, also known by the more prosaic name of *Dirigible No 1*, set off from Farnborough on her first public appearance (she had been test flown four weeks earlier), flew over London, and circled St Paul's before high winds forced her to land in the grounds of the Crystal Palace in Sydenham. Their aircraft was a 120-foot-long airship, filled with 55,000 cubic feet of hydrogen, and powered by a 50 hp engine.

In British military terms, however, Capper and Cody were not the first to take to the air. The Royal Engineers already had a Balloon Corps used for mapping and for aerial reconnaissance, and their tethered balloons had been in limited use since the first experimental flights in 1863. By the 1880s, a school of military ballooning had been established, and extensive use had been made of balloons by the British Army in the Sudan in the 1880s, and in the Boer Wars.

But, of course, the future of aviation lay not in balloons and dirigibles, but in fixed wing craft, developing the ideas of the Wright Brothers, who had made the world's first powered flight on 17 December 1903.

Henri Farman in flight in 1909. Born in Paris to British parents, Farman was one of Europe's most successful pioneer aviators and aircraft designers, achieving many prestigious firsts, including, in November 1907, being the first person in Europe to fly more than a kilometre. In October 1908 he flew non-stop from Buoy to Rheims, a distance of more than 27 kilometres.

HENRI FARMAN.

Above: The American pilot J. Armstrong Drexel flew his Bleriot monoplane to a height of 6,752 feet over Lanark in Scotland on 12 August 1910, but his record achievement was never officially ratified.

Previous pages: Claude Grahame-White at the controls of his aircraft, photographed in Blackpool in 1910. He was given Royal Aero Club's Pilot Licence No 6 on 26 April that year.

Below: Grahame-White flying his Farman aircraft at the Blackpool Flying Carnival, which was held between 28 July and 20 August 1910.

Just over five years after the Wright Brothers took to the air, the first issue of *Flight*, the 'Official Organ of the Aero Club of the United Kingdom', and the world's first weekly magazine devoted to aviation, was still talking about them. For one penny a week, the magazine promised up-to-the-minute news of the rapidly evolving world of aviation. On 2 January 1909 that first issue reported that Wilbur Wright had, two weeks earlier, completed the world's longest flight to date – just short of 100 kilometres – in just under two hours.

Two years later, *Flight* carried a lengthy illustrated account of the 1910 Flying Carnival at Blackpool, with pictures of Drexel, Grahame-White, Tetard, A. V. Roe and others at the controls of their machines. There was, it seems, a lot of prize money to be won, and at the end of the week, Roe had pocketed £50, while Drexel won £175. The outright money winner was Claude Grahame-White, who in a little over one week improved his bank balance by no less than £2,650, an enormous sum in those days! Of that, £650 was prize money: £2,000 was his fee for turning up and giving exhibition flights during the first week of the event.

Tetard and Grahame-White even ran passenger flights – every spectator at the display got a numbered entry ticket, which gave them a 1/500 chance of winning a free flight. Judging by the number of lucky ticket holders who took to the air that week, attendance figures must have been staggeringly high.

A bit of early photo-montage has probably been used here to create a postcard commemorating Frenchman Maurice Tetard's achievement flying his Farman biplane around Blackpool Tower during the second Blackpool Air Carnival in late July 1910. Tetard's flight – circling the tower twice – took place on the last Sunday of the month, two years after an unidentified pilot had become the first to fly around the tower during the Lancashire town's first Aviation Week in 1908. The photograph has been taken from the Central Pier. The postcard was on sale by the end of the first week in August when 'R. M.' wrote to Mr Minto, the Under-Manager of Harraton Colliery in Chester-le-Street, that there was 'nothing but flying machines to be seen at Blackpool this week'.

INDEX